SOCIAL SPACES

VOLUME 1

A PICTORIAL REVIEW

SOCIAL SPACES

SPACES

VOLUME 1

A PICTORIAL REVIEW

ISBN 1 86470 037 8
© 2000
The Images Publishing Group Pty Ltd
Melbourne, Australia 2000
Printed by Leefung-Asco Printers

Contents

Convention Centres and
Entertainment Venues 7

Cinemas and Theatres 41

Libraries 83

Places of Worship 97

Restaurants, Cafés,
Nightclubs and Bars 113

Sports, Activity, Gym and
Clubhouses 167

Other 185

Architects' Biographies 215

Index 221

Acknowledgments 224

Convention Centres and Entertainment Venues

**Brisbane Convention and Exhibition Centre
Brisbane, Qld, Australia**
Cox Architects

1   View with city centre in background
2   External roof detail
3   John Olsen designed floor
4   Street elevation at dusk
Photo credit: Patrick Bingham-Hall

Chinese Cultural Center and Public Library
Ontario, Canada
Kuwabara Payne McKenna Blumberg
Architects

1 Exterior of centre at dusk
2 Display of beautiful ancient costumes
3 Cultural Center's multipurpose area
Photo credit: Kerun Ip

1

2

3

4

5

Virginia Air & Space Center
Virginia, USA
Mitchell/Giurgola Architects

1　View from west showing roofline
2　Entrance from roof into gallery at
　　right-hand side
3　Main gallery from ground at night
4　View from west into gallery from gantry
5　Roofline from galleries

Photo credit: courtesy of The Images Publishing
Group Pty Ltd

The Trocadero
London, UK
RTKL Associates Inc.
1   Model of exterior facade
2   Mult -media tower
3   View of refurbished atrium
Fol owing pages:
   The rocket-shot escalator
Photo credit: courtesy of RTKL Associates Inc.

1

2

Werribee Zoo
Melbourne, Australia
Hassel Group

1 Entrance to zoo
2 Exterior of café's seating area
Photo credit: Blain Crellin Photography

Melbourne Zoo
Melbourne, Australia
Grose Flemming Bate

3 Bear enclosure
Photo credit: Blain Crellin Photography

Fabrimetal
Brussels, Belgium
ASSAR

4 Meeting room
Photo credit: courtesy of ASSAR

3

4

Cairns Convention Centre
Cairns, Qld, Australia
Cox Architects
  1   Front view at dusk
  2   Main foyer upper level
Photo credit: Patrick Bingham-Hall

London Planetarium
London, UK
Fletcher Priest Architects
  3   Exterior view
  4   New perforated hemispherical
       projection system
Photo credit: Peter Smith

Museum of Anthropology
Vancouver, British Columbia, Canada
Arthur Erickson Architectural Corporation
  5   View over artificial lake from the
       northeast
 6&7   Great Hall
Photo credit: Christopher Erickson (5);
Simon Scott (6,7)

Opel Live
Russelsheim, Germany
BDP
  8   Double height entrance hall
  9   Entrance to the 'Tour of the Senses'
 10   Opel Live branding at arrival point
Photo credit: David Barbour

The Chrysler Museum
Norfolk, Virginia, USA
Hartman-Cox Architects
Following pages:
      Interior courtyard
Photo credit: Peter Aaron/ESTO

1

2

3

2

5

6

7

8

9

10

1

Canadian Chancery
Washington, DC, USA
Arthur Erickson Architectural Corporation

1   Reception Court
Photo credit: Timothy Hursley

National Catholic Conference
Headquarters
Washington, DC, USA
Leo A Daly

2   Waiting area
Photo credit: Maxwell McKenzie

Northgate Entertainment Centre
Northriding, South Africa
Frame International

3   Foyer area
Photo credit: courtesy of Frame International

2

3

4

Fountain of Nations
EPCOT Center, Orlando, Florida, USA
WET Design

4   Night view of kinetic jets shooting skyward
     like missiles
Photo credit: Mark Fuller

Joan Sutherland Performing Arts Centre
Penrith, New South Wales, Australia
Cox Architects

5   Street elevation
6   View from park showing tiered levels and
     entry pavilion
Photo credit: David Moore

5

6

2

The Denver Pavilions
Denver, Colorado, USA
ELS/Elbasani & Logan Architects

Opposite:
    Sign wall and escalator from second level retail balcony
2   View from 16th Street Mall
3   View of pedestrian arcade and retail pavilion
4   Day view of bridge over Glenarm Place connecting two retail blocks. Sign wall above.
5   Night view of bridge over Glenarm Place connecting two retail blocks. Sign wall above.
Photo credit: Andrew Kramer

3

4

5

Blue Tower
Brussels, Belgium
Montois Partners with Axia
1   Entrance hall
2   Art gallery
Photo credit: courtesy of Montois Partners

Sydney Exhibition Centre
Sydney, Australia
Cox Architects
Opposite:
    Typical roof cable connection
Photo credit: Patrick Bingham-Hall

1

2

5

6

Sydney Exhibition Centre
Sydney, Australia
Cox Architects

Opposite:
    Upper-level promenade
5   View across gardens
6   Typical mast detail
Photo credits: Patrick Bingham-Hall (1,3);
David Moore (2)

Fountains of Bellagio
Las Vegas, Nevada, USA
WET Design

7   Night view of Bellagio
Photo credit: Ira Kahn

7

Canberra National Convention Centre
Canberra, ACT, Australia
Cox Architects

1   Major office building showing articulated
    facade
2   Hotel frontage to historic park
3   Pedestrian space between offices
4   Hotel atrium
Photo credit: Patrick Bingham-Hall

1

2

3

4

2

3

4

**Star City Casino
Sydney, Australia**
Cox Architects

Left:
    Street arrival
2   View of awning and exterior from roof
3   Exterior from right entrance
Following pages:
    Night view of exterior
Photo credit: Patrick Bingham-Hall

**British Petroleum, Britannic House
Finsbury Circus, London, UK**
Harper Mackay Architects

4   Sinuous flowing curve of main wall
Photo credit: Chris Gascoigne

7

9

10

Crown Casino
Melbourne, Australia
WET Design

11 'Brigade' water and fire towers
12 'Seasons of Fortune' laminar flow and cascade
Photo credit: Ira Kahn

McCormick Convention Center Expansion
Chicago, Illinois, USA
WET Design

13 Exterior water feature and cascade
Photo credit: Ira Kahn

11

12

13

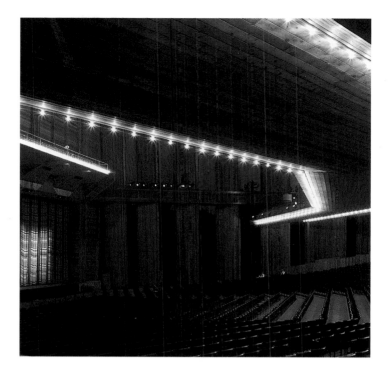

Cinemas and Theatres

**University of North Texas, Lucille 'Lupe' Murchison Performing Arts Center
Denton, Texas, USA**
Hardy Holzman Pfeiffer Associates

1   Winspear Concert Hall chandel ers
2   Winspear Concert Hall detail
3   View from Interstate 35
4   West lobby wall
Opposite:
      Winspear Concert Hall
Following pages:
      Lyric Theater
Photo credit: Craig Blackmon

4

1

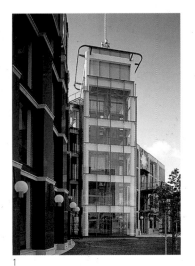

2

3

**Cerritos Center for the Performing Arts
California, USA**

Barton Myers Associates Inc.

1   View of elevator tower
2   View from level two of atrium
3   Elevated view of ceiling
4   Bar
5   View of front entrance to theatre at dusk
6   Main theatre

Photo credit: courtesy of The Images Publishing
Group Pty Ltd

4

5   6

Cambridge Multicultural Arts Center
Cambridge, Massachusetts, USA
Graham Gund Architects
Left:
Elevated view of music room and ceiling rose
Photo credit: Steve Rosenthal

Hoyts Cine 12 at Abasto
Buenos Aires, Argentina
Arrowstreet Inc.
in association with Eduardo Gonzalez

1   Structural columns serve as torchieres in entry
2   Raised wood floor leads to a full bar
Following pages:
Stadium seating maximizes viewing pleasure
Photo credit: Juan Hitters

1

2

Roy Thompson Hall
Toronto, Ontario, Canada
Arthur Erickson Architectural Corporation

1   Foyer area
2   Concert Hall from Choir
Photo credit: Fiona Spalding-Smith

Wolf Trap Farm Park
Virginia, USA
Alfredo De Vido Architects

3   Night view of exterior
4   Night view of interior
Photo credit: Bill Maris

3

1

2

4

Queens Theatre in the Park
Queens, New York, USA
Alfredo De Vido Architects

5   Exterior at dusk
6   Interior of theatre
7   Lobby
8   Interior of theatre
Photo credits: courtesy Alfredo De Vido Architects
(5,6); Norman McGrath (7,8)

The Diller-Quaile School of Music
New York, USA
Alfredo De Vido Architects

9   View of interior of performing space
Photo credit: Norman McGrath

1

Centennial Performing Arts Center, Westminster School
Simsbury, Connecticut, USA
Graham Gund Architects
Previous pages:
 Overall view of theatre
Photo credit: Steve Rosenthal

National Bunraku Theater
Osaka, Japan
Kisho Kurokawa Architect & Associates
 1 Staircase in the east
2&3 View of the stage from the back seat
 4 Main lobby on second floor
Following pages:
 View of the stage from the back seat
Photo credit: Tomio Ohashi

4

2

3

1

**David Eccles Conference Center and
Peery's Egyptian Theater
Ogden, Utah, USA**
Fentress Bradburn Architects

1   Entrance to the newly restored theatre
2   Lobby area of the theatre, finished in muted
    tones and rich gold accents
3   Interior featuring architectural detailing
    and artwork restored to its original
    splendour of 1921
4   Newly restored, 867-seat auditorium
Photo credit: Steve Hall, Hedrich-Blessing

2

3

4

5

6

7

8

9

David Eccles Conference Center and Peery's Egyptian Theater
Ogden, Utah, USA
Fentress Bradburn Architects

5   Interior view of lobby corridor
6&8 David Eccles Conference Center lobby
7   Group Executive training presentation and lecture hall
9   Conference Center lobby
10 Interior view of ballroom

Photo credit: Steve Hall, Hedrich-Blessing

10

1

3

2

4

Yamanami Hall
Kyoto, Japan
Kisho Kurokawa Architect & Associates

1 Overall view from south
2 Looking at the pilotis
3 Andons (standing lights) in the evening
4 Looking at the Andons from second floor roof
5 Corridor to offices with view of skylight
6 Concert Hall
Photo credit: Tomio Ohashi

5

6

1

Nancy Lee and Perry R. Bass Performance Hall
Fort Worth, Texas, USA
David M. Schwarz Architectural Services, Inc.

1   East Great Domes entry
2   Grand lobby, orchestra level
Photo credit: Hedrich-Blessing

3

4

5

Nancy Lee and Perry R. Bass Performance Hall
Fort Worth, Texas, USA
David M. Schwarz Architectural Services, Inc.

3   West Great Domes entry
4   Richardson Room/Founders Room
Photo credit: Hedrich-Blessing

IMAX Theatre
Darling Harbour, NSW, Australia
HBO + EMTB

5   Main entry canopy and foyer glazing
Photo credit: Simon Kenny

5

6

**Nancy Lee and Perry R. Bass Performance Hall
Fort Worth, Texas, USA**
David M. Schwarz Architectural Services, Inc.

5   Founders' concert theatre stage
6   View from stage
Photo credit: Hedrich-Blessing

Sony Pictures European Headquarters
London, UK
Fletcher Priest Architects

1 Stairs to projection room
2 Screening room
Photo credit: Timothy Soar

Screen Cinema
Walton-on-Thames, UK
Fletcher Priest Architects

3 Exterior view of foyer
Photo credit: courtesy of Fletcher Priest Architects

Brooklyn Academy of Music, BAM Rose
Cinemas and BAM Café
Brooklyn, New York, USA
Hardy Holzman Pfeiffer Associates

4 Proscenium cinema, mezzanine level
5 Information kiosk, Donor Wall,
  main entrance/lobby
Following pages:
  Lighting detail
Photo credit: Whitney Cox (4,5); Elliott Kaufmann;
(Following pages)

1

2

3

4

1

2

3

4

5

6

7

8

**Lyric Theatre, Star City Casino
Sydney, Australia**
Cox Architects

1 Theatre auditorium with ceiling by Colin
   Lanceley
4 Lyric Theatre Foyer Drum stair and bar
Photo credit: Patrick Bingham-Hall

**Showroom Theatre, Star City Casino
Sydney, Australia**
Cox Architects

2 Theatre and auditorium
3 Entry and ticket office from casino floor
Photo credit: Patrick Bingham-Hall

**Citizen's Theatre
Glasgow, Scotland**
BDP

5 Foyer with mezzanine gallery and bar
Photo credit: Guthrie Photography

**Amber Hall, Kuji Cultural Center
Kuji, Japan**
Kisho Kurokawa Architect & Associates

6 Entrance Hall in the first floor
7 View from the Entrance Hall ridge
8 Detail of slope and punched metal
Photo credit: Tomio Ohashi

Amber Hall, Kuji Cultural Center
Kuji, Japan
Kisho Kurokawa Architect & Associates
9 View of the main hall from the second
   seating
10 Reverberation equipment used for sound
   absorption
11 Staircase in the east side ascending from
   the main hall foyer to the second level
Photo credit: Tomio Ohashi

9

10

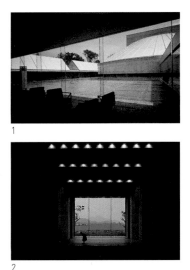

1

2

Sazanami Hall
Shiga, Japan
Kisho Kurokawa Architect & Associates

1&3   View of pond from auditorium
2   Auditorium
Photo credit: Tomio Ohashi

3

Libraries

1

2

3

4

Huffington Library
Culver, Indiana, USA
Hellmuth, Obata + Kassabaum, Inc.

1   Public gallery and third level meeting
     rooms off atrium
2   Detail of piano noble entry
3   Atrium stairwell
4   Detail of corridor area
Photo credit: courtesy of Hellmuth, Obata +
Kassabaum, Inc.

Opportunities and Information Centre
Southall, London, UK
Studiodownie

5   Reception desk
6   Reception desk and waiting area
Photo credit: Peter Cook

Catherine Cookson Reading Room,
University of Sunderland
Sunderland, UK
BDP

7   Catherine Cookson Reading Room
Photo credit: Martine Hamilton Knight

5

6

2

3

French Institute Library
New York, USA
Michael Graves & Associates

1&3   Reference reading room
  2   Second floor lobby
Photo credit: Cervin Robinson

1

Cleveland Public Library
Cleveland, Ohio, USA
Hardy Holzman Pfeiffer Associates
1   'From Here to There' (1997), cast bronze
     reading tables and lighting fixtures by Paul
     O'Keefe

2   The Periodical Center, main building
3   Brett Hall, Main Reading Room
4   Eastman Reading Garden

Following pages:
    Clio and the Death of Hyacinthus, Louis
    Stokes wing
Photo credit: courtesy of Cleveland Public Library
Archives, © Don Snyder (1); Cervin Robinson (2–5)

2

3

4

6

Cleveland Public Library
Cleveland, Ohio, USA
Hardy Holzman Pfeiffer Associates

   6   Eastman Reading Garden
   7   Lending stations, Louis Stokes wing
Photo credit: Cervin Robinson

University of Nantes Library
Nantes, France
Odile Decq, Benoit Cornette

8&10   Entrance hall
9&11   Open space of second floor
Photo credit: Georges Fessy

Film Viewing Library, The Image Bank
London, UK
Studiodownie

  12   Meeting area
Photo credit: Peter Mackinven

Georgetown University Law Center
Library
Washington, DC, USA
Hartman-Cox Architects

  13   Atrium
Photo credit: Robert Lautman

7

8

9

10

11

12

13

Business Development Library & Information Center
London, UK
Studiodownie
1   Reception
2   Library
Photo credit: Peter Cook

Folger Shakespeare Library
Washington, DC, USA
Hartman-Cox Architects
3   New reading room
Photo credit: Peter Aaron/ESTO

Jojima Cultural Center
Fukuoka, Japan
Mitsuru Senda + Environment Design Institute
4   Gallery connecting with hall and library
5   The interior of the library taking in natural lighting from west high-side terrace
6   Foyer in front of hall
Photo credit: courtesy of Mitsuru Senda + Environment Design Institute

Lynn University Library
Boca Raton, Florida, USA
Herbert S Newman and Partners P.C.
7   Screened Arch reading room
Photo credit: Thomas Delbeck

1

2

3

4

5

6

Places of Worship

Sinai Temple
Denver, Colorado, USA
Fentress Bradburn Architects

1   Interior view of lobby showing detail of
    stained glass
2   Interior of entrance lobby
3   Interior view of the central sanctuary
Photo credit: Hedrich-Blessing

**William's College Jewish Religious
Center**
Williamstown, Massachusetts, USA
Herbert S Newman and Partners P.C.

4&6   Closed configuration for Friday services
      and small gatherings
  5   Library
Photo credit: Steve Rosenthal

1

2

3

4

3

6

William's College Jewish Religious Center
Williamstown, Massachusetts, USA
Herbert S Newman and Partners P.C.
Left:
    Chapel
Photo credit: Steve Rosenthal

Mosque and Islamic Cultural Centre
Rome, Italy
Paolo Portoghesi, Vittorio Gigliotti & Sami Mousawi

1   Colonnaded plaza
2   Roof detail
Photo credit: courtesy of The Images Publishing Group Pty Ltd

1

**Chapel for Mt. St. Dominic
Caldwell, New Jersey, USA**
Alfredo De Vido Architects

1   Oculus provides focus

Opposite:
    Overall view of chapel
Photo credit: courtesy of Alfredo De Vido

Colorado Christian Home/Tennyson Center for Children and Families
Denver, Colorado, USA
Fentress Bradburn Architects

1   Interior view of recital hall
2   Interior of the reception area for students and guests
3   Playfully accented interior view of the library
4   Interior view of the cafeteria
Photo credit: Gordon Schenck (1); Nick Merrick (2–4)

Padre Serra Parish Church
Camarillo, California, USA
AC Martin Partners, Inc.

5   View of baptismal and confessional
6   Baptismal and altar viewed through narthex
Opposite:
    Baptismal through narthex to main entry
Photo credit: Aker/Zvonkovic Photography

1

2

3

4

5

6

2

3

4

5

**Battell Chapel, Yale University
New Haven, Connecticut, USA**
Herbert S Newman and Partners P.C.

Previous pages:
    Battell Chapel, Yale University renovation
    and restoration
2   Balcony view of organ
3   View from apse
Photo credit: Norman McGrath

**Community Church of Astoria
Astoria, USA**
Alfredo De Vido Architects

4   Interior of church
Photo credit: courtesy of Alfredo De Vido

**1999 Broadway/Renovation of Holy Ghost
Catholic Church
Denver, Colorado, USA**
Fentress Bradburn Architects

5   Interior view of the cathedral
Photo credit: Nick Merrick

Restaurants, Cafés, Nightclubs and Bars

1

2

3

Popcluster
Tilburg, The Netherlands
Benthem Crouwel Architekten

1&2 Main hall
  3 Sloping floor in main hall
  4 Batcave bar
  5 Small hall
Photo credit: Jannes Linders, Rotterdam

4

5

1

2

3

4

5

6

Battisti Bar
Marina di Ravenna, Italy
Bruno Minardi

1&2 Night view of exterior
3–5 View of interior displaying wainscotted
      bar counter
  6 Entrance area
Photo credit: Marco Buzzoni

1

2

IN-N-OUT BURGER Restaurant
Los Angeles, California, USA
Kanner Architects

1   Detail west elevation

2   Detail of crossed palms
3   West elevation in twilight
4   Detail of interior sign wall
Photo credit: Mark Lohman

3

4

2

Fusebox Restaurant
Atlanta, Georgia, USA
Cooper Carry
Previous pages:
    Seating area
2 Bar
3 Interior of entrance
4 Seating area
Photo credit: Gabriel Benzur

3

4

Fusebox Restaurant
Atlanta, Georgia, USA
Cooper Carry

5&6 Corporate dining room connected to seating area
7 Private dining area
Photo credit: Gabriel Benzur

5

6

1

2

3

4

Coral Bar, Star City
Sydney, Australia
Cox Architects

1 Bar interior
2 View to gaming area
Photo credit: Patrick Bingham-Hall

Big Time Bar, Star City
Sydney, Australia
Cox Architects

3 Bar service area
4 Curving bar interior
Photo credit: Patrick Bingham-Hall

Lightening Ridge Bar, Star City
Sydney, Australia
Cox Architects

5 Overview of interior
Photo credit: Patrick Bingham-Hall

Word of Mouth
New York, USA
Alfredo De Vido Architects

6 Furniture designed by Alfredo De Vido
7 Overview of restaurant
8 View from public hall
9 Interior of restaurant
Photo credit: courtesy of Alfredo De Vido
Architects

Stuarts Restaurant
New York, USA
Alfredo De Vido Architects

10 Bar area
11 Overview of dining area
Photo credit: Paul Warchol

5

7

8

9

6

10

11

1

Monsoon Restaurant
Lebanon, New Hampshire, USA
Arrowstreet, Inc.
in association with Paul Lukez
Architecture

1   Mixing modern sculpture and traditional
    bamboo
2   Restaurant oriented around open kitchen
3   Patio extends restaurant outdoors and
    overlooks pond
4   Upscale design with Asiatic inspiration
Photo credits: Robert E. Mikrut (3);
Greg Premru (1,2,4)

2

3

1

2

3

Restaurant Vau
Berlin, Germany
gmp-von Gerkan Marg und Partner

1   View from Jägerstrabe
2   Emphasis of wooden arch with indirect
       lighting
3   View into the dining hall towards Jägerstrasse
Photo credit: Klaus Fahm

4

Restaurant Vau
Berlin, Germany
gmp-von Gerkan Marg und Partner
4   The 'Coal Cellar' with central bar
5   Staircase to the 'Coal Cellar'

6   High tables on the wall
7   Brown coal briquettes symbolising smoke
8   Stuccoec walls serve as exhibition spaces
Photo credit: Klaus Fahm

5

6

7

8

1

2

3

Lotus Pond Chinese Restaurant, Star City
Sydney, Australia
Cox Architects

1&2 Restaurant interior
  3 Water feature
Photo credit: Patrick Bingham-Hall

Novotel Brussels Centre-Tour Noire
Brussels, Belgium
Atelier d'Art Urbain

4&5 Restaurant
  6 Lobby
Photo credit: Annick Delvigne and Patrick Dupont

M&C Saatchi
Soho, London, UK
Harper Mackay Architects

7 Atrium
8 Café/Informal meeting area
9 Reception area
Photo credit: Chris Gascoigne

4

5

6

7

8

9

10

1

2

13

Bertorellis
Westend, London, UK
Harper Mackay Architects

10   Atrium and dining area
11   A riot of colour, exotic finishes and
     furnishings

12   Display of artwork from Contemporary
     Applied Arts Gallery
     Photo credit: Nicholas Kane

Manhattan School of Music Cafeteria
New York, USA
Alfredo De Vido Architects

13   Interior of cafeteria with view to skylight
     Photo credit: courtesy of Alfredo De Vido
     Architects

Brooklyn Academy of Music, BAM Café
Brooklyn, New York, USA
Hardy Holzman Pfeiffer Associates

Following pages:
     Lepercq Space/BAM Café
     Photo credit: Elliott Kaufman

2

3

4

5

The Crossover Café at 3Com Headquarters
Santa Clara, California, USA
STUDIOS Architecture
Previous pages:
   Roof structure shelters dining and
   adjacent terrace
2   Dining room
3   View of wood-roofed ceiling
Photo credit: Michael O'Callahan

Astral Restaurant, Star City
Sydney, Australia
Cox Architects
4   Bar and casual seating
5   Dining room
Following pages:
   Interior with view to Sydney Harbour
Photo credit: Patrick Bingham-Hall

1

2

3

4

5

6

Halifax plc Headquarters Café
Halifax, UK
BDP

1   Double height ground floor staff café
2   Central bar area lit by suspended glass
    canopy
3   Granite café bar
Photo credit: Dennis Gilbert (1); Martine Hamilton
Knight (2,3)

BT Northern Ireland Headquarters
Belfast, Ireland
BDP

4   Café seating area
5   Ground floor dining area with views to the
    River Lagan
6   Ground floor café servery
Photo credit: Todd Watson

2

3

4

Al Porto Italian Restaurant, Star City
Sydney, Australia
Cox Architects
Previous pages:
    View of interior and ceiling mural
2&3 Dining area
Photo credit: Patrick Bingham-Hall

Pyrmonts Restaurant, Star City
Sydney, Australia
Cox Architects
4 Interior void
5 Internal view
6 Curving exterior details
7 Dining area
Photo credit: Patrick Bingham-Hall

5

6

7

Bangkok Bistro
Washington, DC, USA
STUDIOS Architecture
1 Copper mesh screen detail

Opposite:
   Bar detail
Photo credit: Anice Hoachlander

1

Bangkok Bistro
Washington, DC, USA
STUDIOS Architecture

3   Garden room dining area
4   Bar and front room dining area
5   East side dining with copper mesh screen
Photo credit: Anice Hoachlander

KBC, formerly Kredietbank
Brussels, Belgium
Atelier d'Art Urbain & Michel Jaspers

6   Atrium
Photo credit: Marc Detiffe

3

4

5

The Bistro at 3Com Headquarters
Santa Clara, California, USA
STUDIOS Architecture
Previous pages:
    View of sculptural and rectilinear forms
2   Dining room; use of glazing and natural
    lighting
3   View of terrace dining from Customer
    Briefing Center
4   Displays the use of wide expanse of
    glazing
Photo credit: Michael O'Callahan

2

3

4

5

6

7

8

9

Cyberia Internet Café
Bangkok, Thailand
Bernhard Blauel Architects

5 Computer pods
6 View across café
7 Overlooking café from bridge
8 View along double height screen
9 Stairs to first floor
Photo credit: Somkid Paimpiyachat

1

Lagoon Bar, Star City
Sydney, Australia
Cox Architects

1   Bar adjacent main gaming area
2   Curving bar service area
3   Tropical interior design
Photo credit: Patrick Bingham-Hall

Che Bar and Restaurant
St James, London, UK
Fletcher Priest Architects

4   Bar and wall based light sculpture by
    Martin Richman
Photo credit: Chris Cascoigne

Marconi Communications (formerly FORE
Systems) 53 Bites Café
Warrendale, Pennsylvania, USA
STUDIOS Architecture

5   Exterior glass wall provides natural
    lighting into cafe
6   Adjacent lift modelled after Appalacian
    coal mining 'tipples'
Following pages:
    Features natural lighting, open web trusses
    and exposed HVAC
Photo credit: Richard Barnes

2

3

4

5

2

3

UCB Center
Brussels, Belgium
ASSAR
Previous pages:
    Staff restaurant
Photo credit: Marc Detiffe

AXA Belgium
Brussels, Belgium
ASSAR and Jean-Claude De Wever
2   Staff restaurant
Photo credit: Marc Detiffe

Canteen at 3Com
Dublin, Ireland
STUDIOS Architecture
3   Use of lighting at dining facility
4   Multipurpose 300-seat canteen
Photo credit: Michael O'Callahan

4

Sports,
Activity,
Gym and
Clubhouses

1

2

3

Dainfern Country Club
Johannesburg, South Africa
Head Interiors
Previous pages:
　Salon
Photo credit: courtesy of Head Interiors

Freeman Athletic Center, Wesleyan
University
Middletown, Connecticut, USA
Herbert S Newman and Partners P.C.
1　Field House
2　Natatorium
3　Entry hall
Photo credit: Nick Wheeler

Lois Hancey Aquatic Centre
Richmond Hill, Ontario, Canada
A.J. Diamond, Donald Schmitt and
Company
4　View past stairwell to west facade
Photo credit: courtesy of The Images Publishing
Group Pty Ltd

4

Lois Hancey Aquatic Centre
Richmond Hill, Ontario, Canada
A.J. Diamond, Donald Schmitt and Company
5   Main entrance leading to stairwell and second floor
6   View to beach/patio area and slide pool
7   Base of water slide tower
Photo credit: courtesy of The Images Publishing Group Pty Ltd

6

7

1

2

3

4

Stadium Australia
Sydney, Australia
Bligh Lobb Sports Architecture a Bligh Voller Nield Joint Venture
1   Stadium Australia
Photo credit: Olympic Coordination Authority

Sydney Football Stadium
Sydney, Australia
Cox Architects
2   Stadium at night
3   Evening view highlighting structure
4   Aerial view with city and harbour in background
Photo credit: Patrick Bingham-Hall

Lake Hills Country Club
Seoul, Korea
Michael Graves & Associates
5   Dining room
6   Lobby
Photo credit: Yum, Seung Hoon

Aiwa Golf Clubhouse & Hotel, Miyazaki Course
Miyazaki, Japan
Kisho Kurokawa Architect & Associates
7   Restaurant
Photo credit: Tomio Ohashi

5

6

7

8

9

10

11

Aiwa Golf Clubhouse & Hotel, Miyazaki Course
Miyazaki, Japan
Kisho Kurokawa Architect & Associates

8　Entrance hall
9　Clubhouse lobby
10　Night view of Start Terrace
11　Bedroom suite on 9th floor
Opposite:
　　Opposite: view of sculpture by Noguchi Isamu
　　from restaurant
Photo credit: Tomio Ohashi

The Allen-Stevenson School
New York, USA
Alfredo De Vido Architects

1   Exterior of school
2   Interior of gym
Photo credit: Norman McGrath

Live Oak Community Center
Santa Cruz, California, USA
ELS Elbasani & Logan Architects

3   Lobby
4   Lobby stair and balcony detail
5   Mushroom shower, tots pool
Photo credit: Mark Luthringer

Hamar Olympic Hall
Hamar, Norway
Biong & Biong A/S / Niels Torp A/S

6   Interior of Olympic Hall
Photo credit: courtesy of The Images Publishing
Group Pty Ltd

1

2

3

4

5

6

Fujinomiya Golf Club
Shizuoka, Japan
Kisho Kurokawa Architect & Associates

1   Staircase view toward the lounge on the second floor
2   The lounge on the second floor
Photo credit: Tomio Ohashi

Artezium Arts & Media Centre
Luton, UK
Fletcher Priest Architects

3   Retractable seating in dance studio
4   View from balcony to dance studio
5   Courtyard and 'Light Rain' by Tim Head
Photo credit: Richard Davies

Kyushu Golf Club
Fukuoka, Japan
Kisho Kurokawa Architect & Associates

6–9   Lounge on first floor
Photo credit: Tomio Ohashi

6

7

8

9

1

2

3

Great Southern Stand, Melbourne Cricket Ground
Melbourne, Australia
Daryl Jackson Architects
1   View of stand at dusk
Photo credit: John Gollings

AELTCC
Wimbledon, London, UK
BDP
2   New No. 1 court seats 1,000 people
3   Landscaped hill with big screen for viewing matches
4   New No. 1 court southwest corner
5   Circulation route on the perimeter of new No. 1 court
Photo credit: Charlotte Wood

4

5

Other

Robson Square
Vancouver, British Columbia, Canada
Arthur Erickson Architectural Corporation
1&2 Aerial view from northeast
Photo credit: Ezra Stoller

Universal CityWalk
Los Angeles, California, USA
The Jerde Partnership International
3 Southwest view across street
4 View of street and shop fronts
5 View of framework in atrium
6 North view across street at west end of CityWalk
Photo credit: courtesy of The Images Publishing Group Pty Ltd

3

4

5

6

1

2

3

4

Klassis Hotel
Istanbul, Turkey
Atelier d'Art Urbain

1   Central lobby
2   Nightclub
3   Interior swimming pool
4   Exterior swimming pool
Photo credit: Mehmet Mutaf

Piazza De Gasperi
Bedonia, Italy
Architetto Isotta Cortesi

5   Aerial view of Piazza De Gasperi
6   View of Piazza De Gasperi
7   View of the balustrades and pilasters
    system
Photo credit: Davoli & Buzzoni

Los Angeles Music Center
Los Angeles, California, USA
WET Design

8   Fountain with Jacques Lipchitz sculpture
Photo credit: Ira Kahn

Gas Company Tower
Los Angeles, California, USA
WET Design

9   WaterUnderGlass™ and exterior plaza
Photo credit: Ira Kahn

Seattle International Center
Seattle, Washington
WET Design

10   View of fountain's fleur-de-lis water jets
Photo credit: Ira Kahn

Fountain Place
Dallas, Texas, USA
WET Design

11   Water Gardens in the heart of winter
Photo credit: Ira Kahn

8

5

9

10

11

6

Radisson SAS Hotel
Brussels, Belgium
Atelier d'Art Urbain & Michel Jaspers

1   View of atrium and lifts
2   Atrium
4   Restaurant
5   Overall view of restaurant
6   Bar
7   Lobby
Following pages:
    Elevated view of restaurant
Photo credits: Marc Detiffe (2);
Yvan Glavie (1,4,5,6,7)

Carlton Communications Headquarters
London, UK
Fletcher Priest Architects

3   Restaurant/Café
Photo credit: Chris Casgoigne/VIEW

5

6

7

8

9

1

Galla Placidia N. 5
Ravenna, Italy
Bruno Minardi in association with Simonetta Polano,
Maria Rossi and Lorenzo Zaganelli

1   The exterior and archaeological area of mausoleum
2   View of the interior
3   Connecting portico in the interior courtyard
4   View of the courtyard
Photo credit: Marco Buzzoni

2

3

4

6

7

8

Galla Placidia N. 5
Ravenna, Italy
Bruno Minardi in association with Simonetta Polano,
Maria Rossi and Lorenzo Zaganelli

5&6   The interior
  7   View of the mezzanine
  8   Detail of the mezzanine banisters
Photo credit: Marco Buzzoni

1

Brussels Airport International
Brussels, Belgium
Group 2000 (Bontinck-Jaspers-Montois-
Van Campenhout-Willox)
1   Departure Hall
2   Diamond
Following pages:
    Departure desks
Photo credit: Marc Detiffe

1

2

3

4

5

6

7

8

Brussels Airport International
Brussels, Belgium
Group 2000 (Bontinck-Jaspers-Montois-
Van Campenhout-Willox)

1   Departure desks
Photo credit: Marc Detiffe

PowerGen Operational Headquarters
Coventry, UK
Fletcher Priest Architects

2   Auditorium
3   Auditorium/Restaurant
Photo credits: Peter Cook (2); Timothy Soar (3)

Clark County Government Center
Las Vegas, Nevada, USA
Fentress Bradburn Architects

4   Tree-lined public walkway leading visitors to the kiva-shaped
     main entry lobby
5   Eye-catching details of lobby featuring curved forms,
     overhanding balconies and sculptural lighting fixtures
6   Interior view of public circulation corridor
7   Pyramid-shaped cafeteria and multipurpose area room to serve
     as functional and aesthetic space for employees and visitors
8   Interior view of customer service centre
Photo credit: Timothy Hursley (4,5,7); Nick Merrick, Hedrich-Blessing (6,8)

Mamilla Hilton Hotel
Jerusalem, Israel
Moshe Safdie and Associates Inc.

1 Stone arches in multi-height lobby
2 Enclosed terraced courtyards and arcades
3 Multi-height main entrance lobby
4 Western guest room corridor overlooking entrance courtyard
5 Lounge surrounded by white concrete and stone arcade
6 Contemporary exposed concrete and glass structure
Photo credits: Arndon Bar-Hamma

Banque Indosuez
Brussels, Belgium
Montois Partners

7 Auditorium
Photo credit: Marc Detiffe

1

2

3

4

5

6

7

Biographies

AC Martin Partners, Inc.

AC Martin Partners, Inc. is the oldest, continuously operating family owned architecture and engineering firm in Western United States. Founded in 1906 by Albert C Martin, Snr., the firm has been guided by three generations of the Martin family, providing a continuity of design and management philosophy, goals, and objectives. David C Martin, FAIA, is the Co-Chairman and Chief Designer and Christopher C Martin, FAIA is the Co-Chairman and President.

In nearly a century of practise in Los Angeles, the firm has designed many landmark buildings, including Los Angeles City Hall, the Department of Water and Power Headquarters, ARCO Towers, Home Savings Headquarters, and the Sanwa Bank Building. The firm has also served the needs of aerospace and high-technology industries, having master planned and designed numerous facilities for TRW, Hughes, IBM, Intel, and Hewlett-Packard.

AC Martin Partners, Inc. has been involved in the planning and design of southern California's landmark places of worship including St. Vincent's Church (Los Angeles), St Augustine (Culver City), St. Basil's (Los Angeles), Thomas Aquinas College Chapel (Santa Paula), and Rose Hills Memorial Park (Whittier).

As a fully integrated architecture and engineering firm practising planning, architecture, structural, mechanical, electrical, and civil engineering, AC Martin Partners has a long history of providing a thorough and complete design approach for its clients. By thinking about program, scope, budget, schedule, design and engineering simultaneously, the firm has developed a process for project delivery that results in long-term repeat clients. These clients are the testimony that the AC Martin approach is an enduring one.

AC Martin Partners is headquartered in Los Angeles with offices in Irvine and Sacramento.

Alfredo De Vido

Professional Training includes a Bachelor of Architecture degree from Carnegie-Mellon University, a Master of Fine Arts from Princeton University, and a Diploma in Town Planning from the Royal Academy of Fine Arts, Copenhagen. At Carnegie-Mellon, awards included the American Institute of Architects (AIA) Prize and the Pennsylvania Society of Architects Award.

While on active duty in the U.S. Navy, responsibilities in the 'Seabees' were as Officer in Charge of Construction and Design for the Naval Air Station, Atsugi, Japan.

De Vido is a member of the American Institute of Architects College of Fellows. He has served as a member and chairman of AIA committees and design award juries and has lectured and taught at architectural schools throughout the United States and Canada.

Design awards have been received from national, state, local and city AIA groups the Architectural Record, the U.S. Department of Housing & Urban Development, the City Club of New York, and other professional and trade organizations.

De Vido is the author of three books, 'Designing Your Client's House – An Architect's Guide to Meeting Design Goals and Budgets', 'Innovative Management Techniques for Architectural Design and Construction' published in 1983 and 1984 by the Whitney Library of Design, and 'The Design and Building of Houses' published in 1995 by John Wiley & Sons, Inc.

A monograph on De Vido's work, 'Alfredo De Vido, Master Architect Series III' was published in 1998 by The IMAGES Publishing Group Pty Ltd. Another was published in 1998 called 'Ten Houses. Alfredo De Vido Architects'.

Arrowstreet, Inc.

Arrowstreet Inc. is a multi-disciplined architectural firm founded in 1961 and based just outside Boston, Massachusetts. Arrowstreet's reputation in retail architecture was formed through a series of successful shopping centres across New England, including the acclaimed CambridgeSide Galleria, one of the country's first major urban malls. The firm's expertise in shopping centre design has been recognized repeatedly by the International Council of Shopping Centres (ICSC) which awarded Arrowstreet eight awards for shopping centre design in four years. As the firm has moved from being seen as a regional retail architectural firm to the *architects of choice for commercial development*, Arrowstreet has taken its core expertise and translated it successfully to other building types around the world. Arrowstreet's clients have recognized the firm's skill in adding excitement, life, and value to their properties: whether shopping centres, hotels, or office buildings. Diversification of the firm's work has been increased with the addition of full-service interior design and graphic design groups, which provide an added depth of service to architectural clients and stand alone as independent profit centres with their own client base.

As Arrowstreet has begun to expand and diversify its practice, the company has explored new types of lifestyle retail through the addition of multiplex cinemas and entertainment zones to breathe new life into traditional shopping centres, built up a substantial body of work in the hospitality field with new and renovated hotels in Cambridge and Boston, and established itself in office design with several significant new buildings along the eastern seaboard. Arrowstreet continues to expand its reach outside of New England and further afield internationally, with current projects in South America, Iceland, the Middle East, and China.

ASSAR

Founded in 1985, ASSAR a Brussels-based group, comprises of approximately 70 staff members. As part of the ASSAR group, Global's collaboration ensures that ASSAR may focus on architecture and urbanism, and Global on interior design and facility management.

From the beginning, ASSAR has been one the first architectural firms in Belgium to heavily invest in computer-aided design and conception. Today, projects emerge from three principal sources: new clients, repeat clients and by winning numerous competitions, namely the construction of major administrative headquarters and large scale residential complexes. A permanent dialogue with the client and a constant will to draw quality architecture, results from the management of timing and budgets on both ASSAR and Global's behalf.

ASSAR's work is diverse. It ranges from offices, housing, semi-industrial buildings and laboratories, retail, new buildings and heavy renovations, urban planning, interior design and programming. The architectural style is not pre-set, only a desire to design contemporary architecture where appropriate, and not led by current fashion.

In Brussels, well-known companies such as Axa Belgium (1992 and under progress), UCB (1998), Fabrimetal (1999) or Sofina (under progress) entrusted ASSAR to design their new headquarters. The Assurances du Crédit in Namur, Axa Belgium, IP and Dow Corning asked ASSAR and Global to design working environments and interiors and organize a company's move.

More than 150,000 square metres of office spaces have been completed in the last decade while more than 150,000 square metres of housing are under construction today in several locations in Brussels, apart from the recently completed Royal Military School (2000) for the Belgian Armed Forces, a major development covering 100,000 square meters of new and renovated buildings such as academic buildings, housing, sport centres and offices.

Atelier d'Art Urbain

The Brussels-based, Atelier d'Art Urbain, was founded in 1979 by Sefik Birkiye. Essentially made up of young architects, the Atelier contributes to the improvement of town planning through drafts, architectural competitions, publications and exhibitions. Its members participated to architectural competitions often working jointly with well-known practices in order to be able to present ideas throughout the city.

Atelier d'Art Urbain has been in charge of many diverse projects, including large-scale town planning, small- and large-scale buildings, as well as the fitting out of a boat on the Nile. Atelier d'Art Urbain is also involved in interior decoration, furniture design, luminaries and lighting design.

During the early years, Atelier d'Art Urbain worked jointly with other practices in order to create a synergy that has enabled the firm to participate in larger programs.

Atelier d'Art Urbain is today in charge of several large urban projects, such as administrative complexes (new buildings and renovations), commercial centres as well as hotel and housing programs. The firm has recently completed projects such the renovation of City 2, the largest shopping mall in downtown Brussels and the Novotel Tour Noire, the only major hotel to open in the capital of Europe in recent years. The firm is also well-known for designing major headquarters for companies such as KBC (formerly Kredietbank), Dexia, or Zurich Insurance.

With its main focus to date in Belgium, the firm that has also completed several projects in Turkey, including the Klassis Resort Hotel. It is presently working on the Nile City, a 270,000-square-metre, mixed-used project in Cairo and the Larvotto Hotel in Monte Carlo.

BDP

Building Design Partnership (BDP), was formed in 1961 as a multi-discipline practice of architects, engineers and cost consultants. Its continuing goal is to be Europe's leading building design practice, delivering excellence in design and service through partnership.

The firm has six offices in Britain and Ireland, and a network of European offices under the collective name of BDP International, an association of like-minded professionals across Europe, which today embraces 1,100 people.

BDP is multi-specialist and is therefore active in all the major sectors—urban design and renewal, offices, retail, the arts, leisure, heritage and conservation, healthcare, education, housing, transport and infrastructure.

Creating the built environment requires careful analysis, innovative thinking and the coordinated action of clients, designers, specialist consultants and builders. We design large and small projects with equal enthusiasm, whether it is for a new tennis stadium or a university library. The aim in creating social spaces is to bring people together to be informed or to be entertained.

BDP designs are a direct response to the needs of clients and the community; they combine a concern and sensitivity for the environment, and the people who live and work in it, with an understanding of today's complex buildings. Every project is shaped by the client's aspirations and objectives, as well as by its context. By responding to both clients and contexts, BDP transcends the concept of a 'house style', rooting its architecture in the functional tradition, which holds that form is derived from function.

The practice's continuing objectives for the next Millennium are to create fine work, appreciated by clients, users, public and peers; and to advance the art of creating the built environment.

Fentress Bradburn Architects

Fentress Bradburn Architects was formed in 1980 and has since established a reputation for innovative building design, expertise in construction technology, and excellence in project management. A full service office is maintained with a staff of 85, including 30 registered architects.

The diversity of the firm's work is one of its greatest assets. The principals are currently licenced in 36 states with projects ranging from $3 million to $500 million. In its 19-year history, the firm has completed the design of 35 public sector buildings, 46 office buildings, 4 airport terminals, 40 renovation and preservation projects, 10 museum projects, 61 interior projects and 18 mixed-use residential projects.

Projects include: Clark Country Government Center in Las Vegas, Nevada; Inchon International Airport Passenger Terminal in Seoul, Korea; Colorado Convention Center in Denver, Colorado; National Museum of Wildlife Art in Jackson, Wyoming; Denver International Airport Passenger Terminal Complex in Denver Colorado; the Natural Resources Building in Olympia, Washington; the City of Oakland Administration Buildings in Oakland, California; and the new J.D. Edwards Corporate Campus Buildings in Denver, Colorado.

Fentress Bradburn Architects strives for design excellence. The firm is the recipient of 137 honours, awards and citations for design excellence. These honours include a National AIA Citation for Excellence, Architecture for Justice Exhibition, American Institute of Architects, 1990, and a 1995 Honor Award from the US Department of Transportation for Denver International Airport. The firm was selected as the 1996 Western Mountain Region AIA Firm of the Year. This award recognizes one firm in a six-state region that has continuously produced distinguished architecture over a period of 10 years.

The work of the firm has been featured in over 300 national and international publications. Recent publications of the firms work's are: 'Fentress Bradburn Architects' from AIA's Studio Press; 'Curtis Worth Fentress' from Italy's I'Arca Edizioni; 'The Master Architects Series III: Fentress Bradburn Selected and Current Works'; and Fentress Bradburn Architects' 'Gateway to the West', the latter two both from The IMAGES Publishing Group Pty Ltd.

Hardy Holzman Pfeiffer Associates

Established in 1967, Hardy Holzman Pfeiffer Associates (HHPA) is an internationally recognized architecture, planning and interior design firm. HHPA is highly respected for some of the country's most innovative architecture, particularly for its design of buildings for public use.

The firm continues to be led by its three founding partners: Hugh Hardy, Malcolm Holzman, and Norman Pfeiffer. HHPA has created a reputation for diversity—both in the type of projects completed and in the variety of design solutions employed, which are made in response to the needs and imagery of each project. This versatile aesthetic approach, coupled with HHPA's inquiring attitude, is seldom matched in present American architecture.

The firm's body of work includes such multi-award winning projects as the Bryant Park master plan and design of the Bryant Park Grill; and the restoration of the New Amsterdam and New Victory Theaters. These projects sparked the revitalization of the 42nd Street district in New York. The rehabilitation and expansion of the Los Angeles Public Library's Central Library has won numerous awards including the Lyndhurst Foundation's 'Great American Public Places'; it is the only library in the nation to receive this honour. Other notable projects are the Los Angeles County Museum of Art; the Willard Hotel Office and Retail Complex in Washington, D.C.; the Rainbow Room in New York; new corporate headquarters for Scholastic, Inc.; the Majestic Theater and Rose Cinemas and Café for the Brooklyn Academy of Music; and the expansion and restoration of the Cleveland Public Library.

HHPA's design capabilities have been long recognized throughout the profession. Early acclaim hailed HHPA as leaders in the development of a new, distinctly American architecture. In 1974, the National Institute of Arts and Letters awarded HHPA its Arnold W. Brunner Prize in Architecture. In 1978 the firm received the Medal of Honour from the New York Chapter of the American Institute of Architects, and in 1981 the prestigious AIA Firm Honour Award, the highest single honour that can be bestowed on an American architectural practice. In 1992, the firm's three founding partners were inducted into the Interior Design Hall of Fame. The firm has received more than 100 design awards, including national AIA Honour Awards in 1976, 1978, 1981, 1983, 1994, 1995, 1996, 1997 and 1998.

Herbert S Newman and Partners, P.C.

Founded in 1964, Herbert S Newman and Partners is a collaborative partnership led by Herbert S. Newman, Robert Godshall, Joseph Schiffer, Michael Raso, Richard Munday, Peter Newman and Mavis Terry.

The firm has completed a wide variety of private and public projects throughout the United States, establishing a national reputation for the design of new buildings and the renovation and restoration of existing buildings within several architectural types, including academic, corporate, institutional, religious, and urban design.

The firm is most widely known for its campus architecture: libraries, student centres, residential and dining halls, classrooms, and athletic centres, which can be found at American colleges, universities, and independent and public schools across the country. This expertise in designing collegial settings has also won the firm many corporate and institutional projects.

Since its inception, Herbert S Newman and Partners has dedicated its practice to a humanistic approach to architectural design, having developed an understanding and appreciation of human psychology, behaviour patterns, and community-building through its work with students and clients. The idea that the primacy of space, clarity of path and structure, luminance of natural light, and humanising quality of natural materials are essential in making a lasting, beneficial impact on the built environment in which people live, work, and play, is a tenet of the firm's work.

Having completed a substantial body of urban design projects, Herbert S Newman and Partners has endeavoured to reinvigorate the fabric of the urban landscape, most notably in New Haven, Connecticut. The firm has received over 60 awards for design excellence, and five national AIA awards for design excellence. The firm's work has appeared regularly in architectural journals in the United States and internationally.

Kuwabara Payne McKenna Blumberg Architects

Kuwabara Payne McKenna Blumberg Architects has developed an international reputation for excellence in architeture, urban design, and interior design. The four partners, Bruce Kuwabara, Thomas Payne, Marianne McKenna, and Shirley Blumberg are commited to developing and delivering physical environments that reinforce and express their clients' needs and objectives. The work of KPMB is complex and diverse in both scale and type. It has been recognized for its responsiveness to the urban context as acts and interventions of city building, as well as for its careful, rigorous attention to detailing and technical execution.

The firm has won seven Governor General's Awards for Architecture: Woodsworth College at the University of Toronto; King James Place, Toronto; Kitchener City Hall, Kitchener; the Reisman-Jenkinson Studio/Residence, Richmond Hill; the Design Exchange, Toronto; Grand Valley Institution for Women, Kitchener; and the Joseph S. Stauffer Library, Queen's University, Kingston. KPMB recently won the national competition for the design of the new Canadian Embassy in Berlin, in association with Architects Gagnon, Lettellier, Cyr; and Smith Carter Architects & Engineers Inc.

The office has 11 associates, and a total staff of approximately 55. The members of the firm believe in the value of working on interdisciplinary teams with proficient consultants. They practise architecture at the highest level, and are focused on bringing the work to completion on time and on budget. The studio atmosphere of the office creates a stimulating creative work environment that fosters complementarity and collaboration.

The boundaries between project types of the firm are less critical than the intensity and rigour of design and execution at every scale of the work. If one were to look for a common idea and expression in the work by the firm, it may be claimed that it is a contemporary urbanity and high level of quality and craftsmanship.

Mitsuru Senda + Environment Design Institute

Mitsuru Senda is a professor of Tokyo Institute of Technology, and an honorary President of the Environment Design Institute (EDI) in Tokyo, Japan.

For the past 30 years, he has specialized in designing play structures and play environments for children. He has won several professional design awards and taken a doctorate by a thesis 'The Research of the Structure of the Children's Play Environment' in 1982.

He states: 'specialised design categories such as cities, buildings, landscape, play equipment, and interiors should not be designed separately; they must be designed totally. It is the environmental design.' Based on this policy, when designing a space or area, he values the story—such as history, life, animals, and people—being there, and he introduces himself as 'the environmental architect'. He has wrapped up his design policy into a few publications, one example being Design of Children's Play Environments and is planning to publish two new books: Play Space for Children and Play Structure.

Mitsuru Senda established EDI in 1968. It provides city planning, regional planning, public design, architectural design, landscape design, interior design, products design, and display design from research to design control consistency. EDI has designed parks, museums, children's centres, schools, dwellings and sports facilities.

Montois Partners

With the millennium, Montois Partners is celebrating 50 years of architecture.

Since its inception, the firm brought to Belgium a sense of international style not seen before in the country on such a scale. Since the mid-1980s, to comply with a moving environment, Montois Partners, which remains faithful to the modernistic vision designs a contextual architecture with a revival to the modern movement today.

Projects such as the Hilton Brussels and the research centres of Texaco Europe and Solvay & Cie launched the firm as one of the largest in Belgium. The firm has designed many headquarters office buildings such as Citibank Belgium and Banque Indosuez as well as embassies and has experience in virtually all building types—newly built or renovated ones—including airports.

Montois Partners is probably the Belgian firm, which has the most experience in university and hospital design. The firm has been designing hospitals in Africa and other European countries. It is presently active in Eastern Europe and Turkey.

STUDIOS Architecture

Established in 1985, STUDIOS Architecture (STUDIOS) has developed a diversity of practice that includes master planning, urban design, architecture, interior architecture and strategic planning. STUDIOS has dedicated itself to the pursuit of design opportunities in the civic, institutional and commercial realms, with clients ranging from the University of California to internationally based Fortune-500 corporations.

With offices in San Francisco, Washington DC, New York, London, Paris and Los Angeles, STUDIOS has established a strong international presence with numerous projects underway in the United States, Europe and Asia. The firm has been honoured with more than 70 design awards and has been featured in more than 100 publications for its work around the world.

Current projects include the Milpitas City Hall in Silicon Valley, Wilson Cornerstone's one million square-foot office campus development in San Francisco, interiors for the new Shanghai Grand Theatre and worldwide projects for 3Com Corporation and SGI (formerly Silicon Graphics Computer Systems). Other clients include American Express, Nike, Excite@Home Inc., Andersen Consulting, AirTouch Communications, Tishman Speyer Properties, the Discovery Channel, Sun Microsystems, E*Trade, Young & Rubicam, Warner Bros., Charles Schwab and Cartoon Network.

Index

Index

A.J. Diamond, Donald Schmitt & Company   171, 172, 173

AC Martin Partners, Inc.   106, 107

Alfredo De Vido Architects   52, 53, 104, 105, 111, 126, 127, 135, 178

Architetto Isotta Cortesi   188, 189

Arrowstreet in association with Eduardo Gonzalez   49, 50, 51

Arrowstreet in association with Paul Lukez Architecture   128, 129

Arthur Erickson Architectural Corporation   20, 21, 24, 52, 186

ASSAR   18, 19, 162, 163, 164

Atelier d'Art Urbain & Michel Jaspers   190, 191, 192, 193, 194, 195

Atelier d'Art Urbain   134, 135, 152, 153, 188

Barton Myers Associates   46, 47

BDP   20, 21, 77, 84, 85, 144, 145, 182, 183

Benthem Crouwel Architekten   114, 115

Bernhard Blauel Architects   157

Biong & Biong A/S / Niels Torp A/S   178, 179

Bligh Lobb Sports Architecture
a Bligh Voller Nield Joint Venture   174, 175

Bruno Minardi   116, 117

Bruno Minardi
in association with Simonetta Polano, Maria Rossi
and Lorenzo Zaganelli   196, 197, 198, 199

Cooper Carry   120, 121, 122, 123, 124, 125

Cox Architects   8, 9, 20, 25, 28, 29, 30, 31, 32, 33, 34, 35, 36, 37, 76, 77, 126, 134, 141, 142, 143, 146, 147, 148, 158, 174, 175

Daryl Jackson Architects   182

David M. Schwarz Architectural Services, Inc.   66, 67, 68, 69, 70, 71

ELS/Elbasani & Logan Architects   26, 27, 178, 179

Fentress Bradburn Architects 38, 60, 61, 62, 63, 98, 106, 111, 194, 205

Fletcher Priest Architects 20, 21, 72, 158, 180, 190, 205

Frame International 24

gmp-von Gerkan Marg und Partner 130, 131, 132, 133

Graham Gund Architects 48, 49, 54, 55, 57

Grose Flemming Bate 18

Group 2000 (Bontick-Jaspers-Montois -Van Campenhout-Willox) 200, 201, 202, 203, 204, 205

Hardy Holzman Pfeiffer Associates 42, 43, 44, 72, 73, 74, 75, 88, 89, 90, 91, 92, 135, 136, 137

Harper Mackay Architects 35, 134, 135

Hartman-Cox Architects 20, 22, 23, 92, 93, 94

Hassel Group 18

Head Interiors 168, 169, 171

Hellmuth, Obata + Kassabaum, Inc. 84

Herbert S Newman and Partners P.C. 94, 95, 98, 99, 100, 101, 108, 109, 110, 111, 170, 171

The Jerde Partnership International 186, 187

Kanner Architects 118, 119

Kisho Kurokawa Architect & Associates 56, 57, 58, 59, 64, 65, 77, 78, 79, 80, 81, 175, 176, 177, 180, 181

Kuwabara Payne McKenna Blumberg Architects 10, 11

Leo A Daly 24

Michael Graves & Associates   86, 87, 175

Mitchell/Giurgola Architects   12, 13

Mitsuru Senda + Environment Design Institute   94

Montois Partners   28, 206, 207

Moshe Safdie and Associates Inc.   206, 207

Odile Decq, Benoit Cornette   92, 93

Paolo Portoghesi, Vittorio Gigliotti & Sami Mousawi   102, 103

RTKL Associates Inc.,   14, 15, 16, 17

Studiodownie   84, 92, 93, 94

STUDIOS Architecture   138, 139, 140, 141, 149, 150, 151, 152, 154, 155, 156, 158, 159, 160, 161, 164, 165

WET Design   25, 31, 38, 39, 188, 189

Studio Zacchiroli   194, 195

Acknowledgments

IMAGES is pleased to add 'Social Spaces, Volume 1' to its compendium
of design and architectural publications.

We wish to thank all participating firms for their valuable contribution to this publication
and especially the following who provided photographs for the divider pages:

Contents & Divider Pages

Cox Architects
Star City Casino
Sydney, NSW, Australia
Photo credit: Patrick Bingham-Hall

Hardy Holzman Pffeifer Associates
Cleveland Public Library
Cleveland, Ohio, USA
Photo credit: Cervin Robinson

Herbert S Newman and Partners P.C.
Battell Chapel, Yale University
New Haven, Connecticut, USA
Photo credit: Norman McGrath

Cooper Carry
Fusebox Restaurant
Atlanta, Georgia, USA
Photo credit: Gabriel Benzur

Biong/Biong A/S / Niels Torp A/S
Hamar Olympic Hall
Hamar, Norway
Photo credit: The Images Publishing Group Pty Ltd

Atelier d'art Urbain & Michel Jaspers
Radisson SAS Hotel
Brussels, Belgium
Photo credit: Yvan Glavie